Let's Party!

MICK MANNING AND BRITA GRANSTRÖM

For Chester Fisher

First published in the UK in 2000 by
Big Fish, an imprint of C&B Children's Books,
London House, Great Eastern Wharf,
Parkgate Road, London SW11 4NQ
www.bigfishonline.co.uk

Copyright © Mick Manning and Brita Granström 2000
Design copyright © Big Fish 2000

Editor: Susie Brooks
Designer: Sarah Goodwin

ISBN 1 903174 31 7

British Library Cataloguing in Publication
Data for this book is available from the British Library

Printed in Italy

Dear reader

YOU ARE INVITED TO A ROUND-THE-WORLD PARTY!

HOPE YOU CAN COME!

Come along!

It's time to pack! We're off to some of the most exciting parties in the world! Birthdays, carnivals, festivals and feasts… We're inviting you to join in! Parties shout from the rooftops, 'Today is a special day!' So, what are you waiting for? Come with us!

Let's party!

Please bring:
smiling faces,
singing voices,
clapping
hands,
dancing
shoes…

Just a minute...
What are you wearing?
A party's not a party
if you can't dress up! You'll need to
change as we travel around the world.
Try some of the costume ideas in this
book to help you really look the part!

There are different
sorts of parties and
festivals happening
all year round, all
over the world.

Most festivals
mark special
occasions or
events that people
want to remember.
They give everyone a
chance to celebrate!

This book will take
you on a tour of
some of the livliest
celebrations around!

We've got a year to
cover the world! Where
shall we start? Come
on – turn the page!

Hooray!

The table is covered with all our favourite foods. Look! A cake with candles! Who's blowing them out? There are presents too – and big balloons. Look at our colourful paper hats! We're all singing to one person. Why?

It's their birthday!

Watch out for greedy pets!

6

People all over the world are having birthdays – all the year round! Birthdays celebrate the date you were born. Your birthday is your own special day.

Birthday cakes are traditional in many countries. There's usually a candle for every year you've lived. It's lucky to blow them out all at once, then make a wish!

Play some birthday party games! Pin the tail on the donkey – can you put it in the right place when you're wearing a blindfold?

How old is this birthday boy?

What about musical chairs? Race to sit down when the music stops – and take away a chair each time! If you're the one left standing, you're out. The first person to the last chair wins!

⭐ kung hei fat choy

Welcome to China everyone! Look! A giant dragon is dancing in the street! We're clapping and singing. Firecrackers go POP! They make us jump. People are shouting 'Kung hei fat choy!' 'We wish you riches!' Join the parade…

It's Chinese New Year!

This lively party lasts for 15 days! It celebrates the beginning of the Chinese year. Every year in China is named after one of 12 animals, from the rat or rabbit to the pig!

People give each other money packets, to bring good luck and riches. The envelopes are red and have a message written on the side. Red is a symbol of joy.

Make some lucky money to give to your friends! Cut money-sized pieces from bright paper or magazines, or colour your own with felt pens. Put them in a red envelope with a lucky message on it.

Don't be afraid of the dragon! In China, dragons stand for long life and wealth.

Tangerines are popular New Year presents. Odd numbers are thought to be unlucky, so it's safest to hand them out in pairs.

Firecrackers add extra noise and colour to the buzzing street parades. They frighten away bad luck and evil spirits.

9

La la fiesta!

We're in Brazil. Listen to the rhythm of the carnival band! Look at the amazing, colourful costumes. See the samba dancers! You can sing and dance all day – if you've got the energy! If you get thirsty, drink some coconut milk.

What a carnival!

A carnival costume can take a whole year to make. Which outfit would you choose?

Colourful carnival dancers shimmy along to the sounds of drums and whistles. You can make your own carnival rhythms with wooden spoons and pans for drums. Go on – make some noise!

Carnivals began in Latin America as a last party before Lent – a time when Christians aren't supposed to eat meat. In fact, *carn val* means 'goodbye to meat'!

Pink popcorn and juicy fruits are just a few of the things you can buy here if you're hungry!

Holi is a Hindu festival. It celebrates two stories. One tells of Prahlad, the good son of an evil king. Prahlad was saved by God when his wicked aunt, Holika, tried to burn him on a fire.

People mark Prahlad's story with a bonfire. They burn cow dung on the fire for good luck! Cows are holy to the Hindus, so burning their dung is very special.

The other Holi story tells of the Hindu god Krishna and his girl-friend Radha. Krishna used to playfully spray Radha and her friends with coloured water. Then he'd steal their clothes at bath time!

Whooosh!

Now we're in India. See the painty water flying everywhere! It's in your face and running all over your clothes! We're chasing each other with water pistols and pumps. Soon we'll need to change! Then we'll light a blazing bonfire.

It's Holi!

This coloured spray is made from special powders mixed with water. Imagine what a mess it makes!

For your own bright water fight, fill some squeezy bottles with water and food colouring. Put on some old clothes and play outside!

13

Imagine grabbing a snack while you watch the parade. Try this tasty Japanese omelette!

starry night

This is Japan! See the paper lanterns and streamers, fluttering from bamboo poles! It's getting dark. Listen… Here comes a noisy parade! Dancers and fantastic paper figures are swaying to the clattering of drums and cymbals.

It's Tanabata!

People make model cows in honour of the cowherd star. They use big vegetables for the bodies, and chopsticks as legs. Try making your own! Use dead matchsticks or twigs if you can't find chopsticks.

Tanabata celebrates the legend of two stars: a weaver and a cowherd. The stars love each other, but they live far apart in space. Tanabata marks the one night a year that they meet.

People write poems and make wishes on paper streamers. They hang them from branches to honour the weaver star.

Morning dew and ink powder were once used to write the poems. But most people nowadays buy ready-made ink!

In some places, paper lanterns are set afloat on a river or the sea.

15

When it's dark, the star lanterns will light up the sky, just like the moon!

16

Moon madness!

We're in Vietnam. Look around – the streets are alive with colour! We're breathing in the sweet smell of burning incense. Stalls are selling masks and toys and twinkling star lanterns. High in the sky, the moon is shining bright.

It's Trung Thu!

Make a funny moon mask!

Cut a face shape from a piece of card. Ask someone to help you make two holes for eyes and attach some elastic to go round your head. Now colour your mask with felt pens or stick on some decoration.

Trung Thu celebrates the brightness of the moon. On this night it's full, like a ball, and brighter than at any other time of year.

People eat delicious moon cakes, filled with sugar and egg. The cakes may be shaped like fish or stars or flowers.

Street parades at Trung Thu are bright and lively. Dancers dress up and weave through the crowds. People wear funny masks with faces like animals or demons.

Many families burn incense and light candles in memory of their dead relatives. The smoke that drifts upwards is thought to carry good luck.

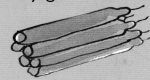

17

Hallowe'en began long, long ago as a way of remembering the dead. It was the night of the year when ghosts came back to earth.

Hallowe'en is most popular in the USA and Canada. Groups of children dress up in scary costumes. They go out 'trick or treating' – asking for sweets and fruit from neighbours' houses.

Pumpkin soup is a tasty way of using up the flesh that's scooped out of the Hallowe'en lantern!

★ Woooaah!

We're at a house in the USA. Listen! There's a rat-a-tat-tat at the door! The door opens. Look! Scary ghosts and monsters are standin on the doorstep! See the swinging pumpkin lantern, gripped in a hairy hand... Spooky!

It's Hallowe'en!

Make a spooky Hallowe'en lantern by hollowing out a pumpkin with a spoon. Get an adult to help you cut holes for the eyes and nose. Ask them to put a candle inside.

Bobbing for apples is a fun Hallowe'en game. You have to get an apple out of a bucket of water using only your teeth! Have a go!

People love to go to fancy dress parties at Hallowe'en! Is that a real ghost?

Fire, fire!

We're in Britain. Can you feel the heat from the bonfire on your cold face? Watch the sparks flying, up and away into the dark! There's a dummy dressed in old clothes, standing in the flames. Fireworks whirl and explode in the sky… Wheeeeeeeeee! BANG!

It's Guy Fawkes night!

The dummy on the bonfire is called a guy. Why not make your own? Collect some old clothes and stuff them with lots of scrunched-up newspaper. Use an old ball or blown-up balloon for the head, and paint on a face.

Guy Fawkes was the leader of a gang who plotted to blow up the English King James, nearly 400 years ago.

The gang planned to set fire to the Houses of Parliament. But they were caught and the king was saved. People were so happy, they held parties with bonfires and fireworks.

Organized bonfire parties are the best! Look! Fire officers are standing by to make sure everything is safe.

Before Guy Fawkes night, children take their guys from house to house, asking for money to buy fireworks.

Traditional foods include sticky treacle toffee, baked potatoes and toffee apples.

⭐ Burning bright

We're out on the streets of an Indian town. Can you see the tiny lamps, glowing against the dark night sky? Watch the cheeky tigers, leaping and growling!

It's Diwali!

Diwali is short for *deepavali*, meaning 'row of lights'. It's a time of celebration for both Sikhs and Hindus. All over India, people burn tiny clay lamps around their homes.

During Diwali, people pray mostly to Lakshmi, goddess of wealth. But other gods may be worshipped too. This Diwali card shows Ganesh, god of wisdom.

These children are dressed up as tigers in honour of the god Vaghaveda.

Why don't you be a tiger dancer too? Cut out a thin band of card that fits around your head. Paint it orange and black, then staple on some painted card ears. Ask someone to colour your face with face paints – then prowl around like a big cat!

Diwali lasts for two whole days. On the second night, people feast, pray and light noisy fireworks.

Hanukkah is the Jewish festival of light. It celebrates a miracle that happened at the Temple of Jerusalem more than 2000 years ago.

The lamp oil in the Temple had almost run out. But amazingly it gave light for eight whole nights! People remember this by burning candles on a special pronged candlestick during Hanukkah.

You might get eight presents during Hanukkah – one for each day of the festival!

Happy holiday!

We're with a family in the USA. It's nearly time to eat. Smell the hot potato cakes and sticky doughnuts, fried in oil! We're playing games and opening presents. Look at the giant candlestick, lighting up the room!

It's Hanukkah!

Make a Happy Hanukkah card! Take a piece of red or black paper, any size you like. Fold it in half, then carefully draw on the candlestick shape with a glue pen. Sprinkle glitter over your design, then shake the card over newspaper. Write a message inside!

Dreidl is a traditional Hanukkah game. Players spin a top and can win or lose chocolate money.

Latkes are savoury cakes made with potato, onion, flour and egg. They're fried in olive oil and eaten with sour cream and apple sauce.

⭐ Winter white

Now we're in Sweden, deep in wintertime. Outside, all is frozen and snow is falling, but inside we're warm and cosy. Look! Here comes a procession, parading around the school. We're going to eat buns and drink hot chocolate – come on!

It's Santa Lucia!

Star wands are carried by the 'star boys' on Lucia day. To make a wand, cut out a star shape from shiny paper. Stick it on to card and fasten it to a rod with sticky tape.

Don't worry about burning your head! The candles on the Lucia crown run on batteries.

This party is held for St Lucia, the Swedish saint of light. It happens on one of the longest nights in winter, close to Christmas.

The leader of the Lucia parade wears a beautiful crown of candle-shaped torches on her head. Other children carry lanterns in honour of the saint.

People hang gingerbread figures all around the house. They eat *lussekatts* – special buns made from sticky saffron dough, dotted with juicy raisins.

Christmas is a Christian festival which celebrates the birth of Jesus. School children dress up and act out the story, which is called the Nativity.

Shepherds and wise men carried gifts to the baby Jesus. Presents at Christmas time are a fun reminder of this!

People once thought pine trees and holly were magic because they stayed green all winter! The tradition of having a family Christmas tree began in Germany.

In some places, a kiss under a piece of green mistletoe is thought to be very lucky!

Silent night

Hush! We're watching a school play in Germany. Look – a golden star, angels and a baby doll! At home there's a prickly tree, sparkling with shiny decorations. Presents are waiting to be opened. Pull your cracker – SNAP! It's got a joke, a hat and a gift inside!

It's Christmas!

When Jesus was born, angels appeared to shepherds to tell them the exciting news. Why not dress up as an angel? You'll need to wear something white, like a white nightie. Ask an adult to help you make some wings out of card and some loops of ribbon or wire.

The Nativity took place in a stable.
Look at the farm animals, standing
around the mother Mary!

Hoo haa!

We're in Scotland, on the Shetland Isles. It's a cold, dark, winter's night. But look! Here comes a torchlight procession. People are dressed as Vikings and burning a wooden ship! It's way past bedtime, but there will be dancing long into the night…

It's Up Hellya!

Pretend you're a Viking! Fasten a towel or scarf around your shoulders for a cape, then put a plastic bowl on your head as a helmet. Make a sword out of stiff card, then paint it, or cover it with shiny silver foil.

The Vikings ruled the Shetlands a thousand years ago. The Islanders remember their history with this merry midwinter festival.

A torchlight procession honours the warrior Vikings. It ends with a blazing bonfire to warm people up from the cold.

Up Hellya is a really noisy party!
Can you hear the people shouting?

The burning boat is a copy of an old Viking longship.

⭐ A festival year

See how we've filled a year with parties! And these are just a few of the world's celebrations. We haven't had time to visit them all – but there's always next year!

January
New Year
Up Hellya (Shetland Isles)
Australia Day

February
Chinese New Year
Carnival (Christian)

March
Purim (Jewish)
Holi (Hindu)

There's probably a party going on somewhere every day!

June
Midsummer (Sweden)

May
Wesak (Buddhist)
May Day (Europe)

April
Baisakhi (Sikh)
Passover (Jewish)
Easter (Christian)

Many religious festivals don't have a fixed date. They may happen at a different time each year!

Tanabata (Japan)

July
Independence Day (USA)
Obon (Japan)

August
Esala Perahera (Buddhist)
Raksha Bandhan (India)
Eid ul-Fitr (Muslim)

The dates of Muslim festivals change the most.

November
Guy Fawkes Day (UK)

October
Diwali (Hindu/Sikh)
Hallowe'en

September
Trung Thu (Vietnam)
Rosh Hashanah (Jewish)

Try making your own party calendar! Where does your birthday come in?

Day of the Dead (Mexico)
Thanksgiving (USA)

December
Hanukkah (Jewish)
St Lucia (Sweden)
Christmas (Christian)